Made in the USA
Monee, IL
24 March 2021

63650504R00072